# Elisabeth Jesus de Souza

# Love as a Pedagogical Component

Elisabeth Jesus de Souza

# Love as a Pedagogical Component

## A loving look at early childhood education for socially vulnerable children

ScienciaScripts

**Imprint**

Any brand names and product names mentioned in this book are subject to trademark, brand or patent protection and are trademarks or registered trademarks of their respective holders. The use of brand names, product names, common names, trade names, product descriptions etc. even without a particular marking in this work is in no way to be construed to mean that such names may be regarded as unrestricted in respect of trademark and brand protection legislation and could thus be used by anyone.

Cover image: www.ingimage.com

This book is a translation from the original published under ISBN 978-613-9-71903-7.

Publisher:
Sciencia Scripts
is a trademark of
Dodo Books Indian Ocean Ltd. and OmniScriptum S.R.L publishing group

120 High Road, East Finchley, London, N2 9ED, United Kingdom
Str. Armeneasca 28/1, office 1, Chisinau MD-2012, Republic of Moldova, Europe
Printed at: see last page
ISBN: 978-620-7-72430-7

*What to do with the old certainties? At the moment I feel that they only serve as a starting point and not as an arrival point.*

Margareth Martins de Araújo

## ACKNOWLEDGEMENTS

I thank God for everything he has given me; for being the Lord of my life.

To my honourable parents Sebastião Barbosa de Souza and Laudelina Maria de Jesus, my four brothers, my six sisters, in short, to my family for giving me the basis to face life's obstacles, especially to my brother Milton de Jesus, his wife Maria Aparecida de Jesus and their daughters, who helped me to come and stay in Niterói.

The Church, which has given me all the support I need.

My friend Zulma Blanco Queiroz

To my very dear supervisor Margareth Martins de Araújo, who has been a support in my academic journey since graduation and a living example in human relations, without ever hesitating to guide me; through whom my encounter with Social Pedagogy took place.

To my dearest referee, Elionaldo Fernandes Julião, who, when observing my mistakes, never disregarded my successes; who, since our academic meeting, has also co-operated in my progress and development in academic and professional life, through his guidance and suggestions.

To all the teachers, who generously gave part of their precious time to the course, co-operating with our training.

To Antônio Wanderley, the most worthy employee of the Post-Lato Sensu Programme Secretariat, who never hesitated to cooperate in the smooth running of the Social Pedagogy for the 21st Century course.

To the entire team at the Professor Nilo Neves Municipal Early Childhood Education Centre: teachers Maria Esther, Eliane Felix, Eliane Torres and Cristiane; headmasters Maria Aparecida and Maria Emília; coordinator Marcelo; pedagogue Marineth; cooks Sueli, Andréia, Meirely and Joana; cleaners Seu Evaldo, Verônica, Angélica and Flávia; security guard Cleilson.

To all the families who may or may not be in a situation of social vulnerability, but who entrust us educators with the possible change in their children's lives through our pedagogical actions.

To all the educators who have been looking for ways to realise a transformative and liberating education in the daily lives of their students.

## SUMMARY


**Chapter 1**                              **14**

**Chapter 2**                              **28**

**Chapter 3**                              **41**

# INTRODUCTION

Coming from a working class background, more precisely from the countryside, the daughter of an illiterate mother and father, I saw school as something good from an early age. And my parents thought so too, because they said that my brothers and I needed to study. I went to school for the first time at the age of seven. I don't remember how it went, but I do remember that at the end of the day, under a tree, where the whole family used to gather almost every day, at dusk my father, after a day's work under the sun, sat down in front of me and asked if I had liked school and the teacher. Although he spoke very little, I always saw in him, my father, in his attitudes towards me and my siblings the concern of a responsible family man; difficulties were not the limit for him, he put his feelings as a father above them, he made no effort to protect us. One look was enough for me and my brothers to understand what he meant. In order to defend us from evil or ill-intentioned people, he was capable of going beyond any limit, no matter what anyone thought of him; it didn't matter what people thought of him, my safety, my life and that of my brothers was what really concerned him, and if necessary, he was always prepared to fight for us. Imagine what it was like for him and my mum to see us leaving the house to go to school, having to cross rivers and forests, passing by unknown people (with whom we shouldn't stop to talk). Another factor that worried them was the weather; the flooding period was a threat to our lives, because the rivers would overflow and the waters would gain voracious force, often the heavy rain would come and we would be at school, so the risk was inevitable, my father would wait for us on the way to help us cross, he knew the tricks to go against the force of the water. Sometimes we learnt about the changes the rivers had undergone, so we would return by another route. When the rain came and we were still at home, depending on its strength, we couldn't go to school.

I remember a happy and healthy childhood with my ten siblings, that's right: I have four brothers and six sisters; I'm the eighth of them all and the fourth of the girls. I was born on the Serrinha farm, in the interior of Espírito Santo, where my father worked as a farmer, surrounded by forests, mountains, rivers, animals and far from urban life, and I lived there until I was about twelve years old. A childhood lived. I didn't have dolls. In fact, I'm sorry, I did have dolls: my sisters and I used to make our own dolls, out of clay or wood; we also had corn dolls, in all different colours. Through them, nature also expressed its diversity and beauty, as well as its generosity. We weren't influenced by television, because we didn't have it. These details were no obstacle to our happiness. While my father took care of the coffee, my mother and older siblings planted and harvested on another part of the land given to them by Mr Carlos, the owner. This portion was for our own consumption, to help with household expenses; we also raised cattle for the same purpose. The domestic education we received gave us the basis to leave the door to happiness open. My mother's faith never allowed us to perish in the midst of the difficulties that life continually presented us with. Unlike my father, my mother almost always used the rod when necessary. As the main educator in the family, she wouldn't be able to educate eleven children with her gaze alone, so dialogue (which was rarely used) came hand in hand with the rod. As well as taking care of her children's domestic upbringing, my mother had other responsibilities, as already mentioned. I would also like to express my immense gratitude to my very worthy older siblings, who always added to the family context. My eldest sister took charge of the household with great responsibility.

I was given values that are part of me today, which help me to overcome barriers and obstacles in life: unanimity between us siblings was something that had to prevail; whenever we had a fight my mum would put us on our knees to pray to God (we prayed the Our Father) and ask for forgiveness for each other; at school we had a duty to defend each other with all our strength and voracity; we shouldn't pick fights with our classmates, not even if we were provoked; the teacher was the authority, we owed her respect and obedience. But if any of us were to be the target of injustice, we had to be defended by the other siblings. We always kept an eye on each other to make sure no one touched us. Every day when we woke up to go to school, my mum already had the milk boiled so that my brothers and I could drink it before going out; my older brothers woke up earlier to take the milk from the cows. And while we woke up, my mum would prepare our breakfast. We walked a long way to get to an urban perimeter, where we went to primary school. The nearest neighbours were about twenty minutes from my house, but they didn't have children. We walked for another twenty minutes and spotted the next neighbours, where we eventually found other children.

I remember many times seeing my mother sharing what we had with the neighbours. If someone passed by our house, they would certainly stop to chat with her, and she would invite them in for a coffee; usually time would pass and that coffee would last, and she and my father would chat with the visitor, who would forget about time. Visitors were almost always served: coffee, curd cheese, beiju (made in the wood-fired oven, the same oven in which the manioc flour was roasted), cassava, sweet potato, puba cake or cornmeal cake. If the visit lasted until lunch or dinner, I would certainly eat a free-range chicken or fish; if not delicious pork, I would hardly eat duck meat; but turkey was a great possibility. The oxen looked like they were going to be left for seed.

My parents, especially my mother, always believed that it was God who provided us with what we needed, so they never refused to reach out to our neighbours; they said that we didn't know about tomorrow, that we would also need others. This was true; whenever we needed it, we could count on good neighbourliness (even if the nearest neighbour was a few kilometres away). Often on our way home from school, my brothers, sisters and I would stop at our grandparents' house to eat, so we could continue on our way to our house.

School made me dream. The teachers seemed to like me and believe in my intelligence, even though I didn't have that discernment or understanding. I remember two of them always telling my mum that I was intelligent. They said to me: You're very clever! In order for them to repeat their words, I did all my homework. Teachers Lecy and Juvenil made a loving and welcoming contribution to my belief in the importance of education in the life of a citizen. And I was a child of dreams. As I came to understand things and society, I realised that life is full of obstacles. For some, these obstacles are milder, but for others they are violent and often disrespectful and inhumane. I was awakened to have this understanding, to do this reflective exercise, and to realise this social and purely capitalist logic when, at the age of fifteen, I left my parents' home and went to the city to work as a domestic servant in order to study. That's how I created strategies and travelled paths.

With the limitations that the rural context presents in terms of professional opportunities, it would have been impossible to realise my dream of continuing to study and expand my systematised knowledge. So at the age of fifteen I asked my parents to let me go to the city to work and study, and so I went to work as a maid in the house of someone known to the family, in Vitória da Conquista, BA, far away from the family, whom I only visited every year. I lived there for nine years, finished secondary school and returned to Espírito Santo to live with my parents. But now I wanted to study for a degree. I already lived in the city, but the chance of access to a public university was almost nil, simply because of the absence of one in my town.

In August of 2014, at the age of twenty-seven, I moved to the city of Niterói, Rio de Janeiro, where my brother and his family already lived. A group of young people from my church encouraged me to study and enter a public university, preferably the Universidade Federal Fluminense. They took me to a pre-university entrance exam course at the Faculty of Education of the university I wanted to attend. In two thousand and seven, at the age of twenty-nine, I passed both stages of the selection process at the Fluminense Federal University for the Pedagogy course. I started studying in the second semester of the same year.

Often some classes seemed like mere discussion, without coherence. At other times, the lecturers seemed sincere, truthful in their speeches, but how could they make what they said tangible? Everything seemed to be nothing more than a utopia, sometimes I got confused, I didn't see any link between theory and practice. When I was in my fourth term, I met a teacher who helped me realise that it is possible to practise what you say; she wasn't talking about someone else's practice, but her own. Her lessons were mixed with her own experience of daily school life over the years; that was the weight of her testimony. As I got closer to the teacher Margareth Martins de Araújo, of whom I am speaking, I began to understand my insertion into the so-called intellectual context; my being there now seemed to begin to make sense. Since childhood I was taught that to conquer another space in society is to be "better", to be "someone in life"; that if I wanted to be that someone I would have to study a lot, in other words, what I was, the ethical and moral values that came from my family and faith; the knowledge that

I was acquiring as a being under construction throughout my life, had no value for the system; me, my existence didn't mean much, it didn't add up in society if I didn't become that socially pre-requisite "someone". And that's how capitalist society convinces you to think, and you automatically mould yourself, or are moulded, to this hegemonic and dominant thinking of the system, submitting without any question. However, back in my childhood, when I dreamed of achieving things, it wasn't part of that dream to deny my origins, to deny my family, to deny myself.

My meeting with Margareth Martins was a kind of salvation. As an organic intellectual, she showed me, through her work, how to deconstruct this mistaken thinking: that human value is recognised by one's social status, that one who has a university degree, for example, is a winner. It was on this path to liberation that I had an encounter with Social Pedagogy through this intellectual, and I became part of and an integral member of the "PIPAS" research group, coordinated by her.

In two thousand and fourteen, having already completed my degree, I passed the selection process for the Postgraduate Course in Social Pedagogy for the 21st Century, also coordinated by Margareth Martins de Araújo. As I continue to research my own practice as an educator working in the classroom, I realise how necessary it is for social educators to be present in the school context of boys and girls in situations of social vulnerability. It was in this relationship, in this encounter with Social Pedagogy, that I became an educator who was not only critical and questioning, but also willing to learn love.

The title of this work, AMOROSIDADE COMO COMPONENTE PEDAGÓGICO (LOVE AS A PEDAGOGICAL COMPONENT), I borrowed from an article of my own, published in the magazine UDZIWI; the same title also represents one of the chapters of the concluding work of the Specialisation Course in "Social Pedagogy for the 21st Century", held at the Fluminense Federal University, Niterói, Rio de Janeiro, between 2014 and 2016, entitled "SOCIAL PEDAGOGY: A loving look at early childhood education for boys and girls in situations of social vulnerability". The work was revised (including its title) and transformed into a book, the work developed here. All the research carried out during this period is included in this book.

Accepting the proposal to develop this theme is a challenge. Although I won't be talking about anything other than my own teaching practice, conveying what you feel, your own feelings through writing, is no easy task. Accepting the invitation as a first step also means overcoming the first obstacle in this decision.

It was my own work in the classroom with two-year-olds, as a teacher, in a community located in one of the neighbourhoods of Niterói, RJ, during the same period in which I did my specialisation, that motivated me to choose this topic.

As I observe such young children entrusted to us teachers, I am deeply interested in the issue of loving kindness. I am motivated to dedicate hours of my days, from Monday to Friday, every week to these little ones who are separated from their families from a very early age, every day for long hours. So I began to research my own practice. And if childhood is in constant movement, when we think about it we must also consider our educational actions in relation to this childhood, which is changing and being built all the time

I'm talking about an audience with its own peculiarities: children in situations of social vulnerability. This requires us educators, who still believe in education, to have a loving and hopeful outlook. For many, talking about love is not an easy task, as it requires sensitivity, courage and practice. Practising how to look, what to look at and why to look is an exercise that requires constant reflection.

In developing this theme, I want to see, through research and my own practice, my experience of working in the classroom, and through some authors and their works, the possibility of changes and transformations in the school and daily life of these children who live on the margins of society, through the exercise of love; to motivate educators who are involved and committed to the educational process for children, to bring about changes in their teaching practice without neglecting the issue of love and affection, certain that exercising love is not to be confused with a loss of authority, thus providing freedom of expression in relation to relevant issues; to awaken in myself, first and foremost, a way of thinking that is free of prejudices, a purely human and loving view of this audience; to present relevant contributions from Social Pedagogy that can help educators understand the need to build an affective link between teachers and their students. The aim of social pedagogy is for the vulnerable to be included in the practices and proposals of education policies.

Discussing this topic is important because although the issue of love has already been discussed by some authors in their works and is already the practice of many teachers, love is still a stumbling block in the daily lives of many other educators. It's important that we education professionals have the courage to assume that we believe in the power of expressing love and affection in the teacher-student relationship, especially in the early childhood education of children in situations of social vulnerability. Another point that led me to consider the choice of topic relevant is that this is a topic that is rarely addressed in lectures on education, cycles of conversations involving educational issues and pedagogical meetings.

The research method used was participant observation. As I worked as a teacher and took an active part in the daily lives of the children in question, I engaged in dialogue with my own practice and observed it, always questioning myself as a professional and as a human being, as well as seeking dialogue with professional colleagues.

It is important to highlight some of the authors and their respective works used as a theoretical basis. They are: Paulo Freire - "Pedagogy of Autonomy: knowledge and pedagogical practices"; Léo Buscaglia - "Love": Margareth Martins de Araújo - "Social Pedagogy - Dialogue with working children".

Paulo Freire was born in Recife, Pernambuco, on 19 September 1921. He graduated in Law from the Recife Law School. He was concerned about the large number of illiterate adults. Because of his commitment to teaching the poorest, he created a method based on the vocabulary of each region. He became an inspiration to generations of teachers, especially in Latin America and Africa.

His first experiments took place in Rio Grande do Norte in 1963, when he taught 300 adults to read and write in 45 days. His educational project was linked to the government's developmentalist nationalism
João Goulart, but his career in Brazil was interrupted by the military coup of 31 March

1964. Accused of subversion, he spent 72 days in prison and then went into exile. In Chile, he worked for five years at the Chilean Institute for Agrarian Reform (ICIRA). During this period, he wrote his main book: "Pedagogy of the Oppressed" (1968).

In 1969, he taught at Harvard University (United States) and in the 1970s he was a consultant for the World Council of Churches (WCC) in Geneva (Switzerland). During this period, he gave educational advice to the governments of poor countries, mostly on the African continent, which were going through a process of independence at the time.

At the end of 1971, he made his first visit to Zambia and Tanzania. He then went on to play a more significant role in education in Guinea-Bissau, Cape Verde and São Tomé and Príncipe. He also influenced the experiences of Angola and Mozambique. In 1980, after 16 years in exile, he returned to Brazil, where he wrote two books considered fundamental to his work: "Pedagogy of Hope" (1992) and "In the Shadow of this Mangueira" (1995). He taught at the State University of Campinas (Unicamp) and the Pontifical Catholic University of São Paulo (PUC-SP). In 1989, he was Secretary of Education in the Municipality of São Paulo under Luíza Erundina.

An honorary doctorate from 27 universities, Freire received awards such as Education for Peace (from the United Nations, 1986) and Educator of the Continents (from the Organisation of American States, 1992). He died in São Paulo on 2 May 1997.

About Léo Buscaglia (Felice Leonardo Buscaglia - 31 March 1924 - 12 June 1998).

Buscaglia was an Italian-American teacher and writer, one of the greatest writers of recent times, who wrote about love. His books changed the way many people saw love, always emphasising the idea of living in the moment, expressing the love you feel for someone and not creating expectations. His first book "Love". There were several authors in various countries, all copying and imitating the style of Leo, the forerunner of all this. Before his death, he created the NGO Felice, dedicated to helping the needy around the world. He died at the age of 74 on 12 June 1998 of a heart attack while sleeping at his home in Lake Tahoe, California. He visited Brazil once, in 1995, where he gave a series of lectures. He lectured at the University of Southern California, USA, and was the author of articles for The New York Times on subjects related to love at the university itself.

From this illustrious author I'm going to use the aforementioned work: "Love". It is a work that tests and conquers the heart and sensitivity of the reader, especially if you are an educator capable of loving, who believes in the action of love. He presents us with an infallible path: the path of love; on this path we will be able to touch each other through the heart, through the freedom to love, we will realise that we are interdependent beings. Through this mutual help, the book also leads us to share what we have with each other; in this process there is no loss, but multiplication. It speaks of love as the greatest miracle belonging to the human being.

Margareth Martins de Araújo has a degree in Pedagogy from UERJ (1989), a Master's in Education from UFF (1998) and a PhD in Education from UNICAMP (2005). She is currently an associate professor in the department of Society, Education and Knowledge at the Faculty of Education of the Fluminense Federal University (FEUFF). She coordinates the Social Pedagogy and Educator Training research group (PIPAS - CNPq 2006). She coordinates the project Urban Child Labour: myths and challenges, the Extension Course in Social Pedagogy for the 21st Century (PROEX, 2005), and the Teaching, Research and Extension Group for the Initial and Permanent Training of Educators of Children in Situations of Social Vulnerability (GRUPO PIPASUFF). She is the coordinator of the Specialisation Course in Social Pedagogy at FEUFF, was the Coordinator of the Pedagogy Course at the Federal University - Niterói, was a lecturer at the University of Greater Rio (UNIGRANRIO), was the coordinator of the Specialisation Course in Management of Pedagogical Work at UNIGRANRIO, and is a member of the group of lecturers on the Specialisation Course in Inclusive Special Education, she was a UNESCO consultant for Early Childhood Education and Daycare, a consultant for Social Assistance Institutions in Niterói, Rio de Janeiro and Duque de Caxias associated with CEPEMISA - Instituto de Ação Social, a collaborator in the Family School Project of the Niterói Court for Children, Youth and the Elderly from 2010 to 2014.

Consultant to the Rio de Janeiro Court for Children, Youth and the Elderly in 2014. Member of the Education, Society and Spirituality Research Centre (NEPES).

I'd like to take advantage of this author's work "Social Pedagogy". Through the author's own practical experiences, this work presents alternatives and possible ways of building and learning in the educational context. It presents Social Pedagogy as the pedagogical component directly responsible for the inclusion of children in situations of social vulnerability in the school world.

# CHAPTER I

## Early Childhood Education and Social Vulnerability

In this chapter I intend to discuss the concept of Early Childhood Education and Early Childhood Education for the Vulnerable. But in order to understand these concepts, we need to question our conception of childhood. And what is our conception of education? Talking about childhood also means talking about rights and achievements. With the support of the LDB of 20 December 1996 and a number of authors, I have come up with some thoughts that lead us to a common answer.

## 1.1. Concept of Early Childhood Education

> *The purpose of early childhood education, the first stage of basic education, is the integral development of children up to 5 (five) years of age, in their physical, psychological, intellectual and social aspects, complementing the action of the family and the community.* (National Education Guidelines and Base Law)

In the educational context, we can consider that the integral development of the child comes from the understanding that education, being a formative process, cannot refrain from its responsibility to co-operate in the child's full development. Logically, we understand that we are talking about the child and their whole being. This means that for this objective to be achieved, we need to be concerned with the childhood of boys and girls in all its aspects.

When dealing with the physical aspect of children in early childhood education as part of their integral development, we must realise and pay attention to some basic and necessary care. One of these is bathing, feeding and health, for example. I think that these moments should be given more importance by us educators working in early childhood education. Why should we? Because it's human, it's part of loving your child, it's part of caring. Look at the look of satisfaction and joy on the faces of the little ones when they get out of the bath. Bathing is part of the process of humanising the individual.

Leonardo Boff (1999, p.98) helps us when he says that: "care enters into human nature and into the constitution of the human being. Without care, the human being becomes without resistance, exhausting himself and losing the meaning of living". The author under discussion sees care as an important tool for educators to persevere in their teaching practice. He says that in care lies the cure for humanity.

The verb to care takes on a broad meaning when it is transferred from being just a verb to becoming a subject in constant action. This care requires that instead of loneliness there is human warmth, that we smell each other's scent, perceive the colour of each other's hair, the touch of each other's skin, making life a good and acting uprightly in our actions. Caring leads us to self-criticism and a new paradigm for human coexistence.

The following is an account of teacher Maria Esther's experience:

> Danilo was two (2) years old; most of the time he came into the classroom with a certain smell that wasn't very pleasant. Hugging him in this condition made me uncomfortable, but I made no distinction between him and the other children, so I never stopped hugging him. Whenever possible, we would bring his bath time forward, taking care not to cause him any embarrassment. We would then look for something concrete to justify his taking a bath at that time. Danilo's satisfaction was evident on his face after his shower. Sometimes his clothes in his rucksack were still damp. Perhaps this was because Danilo had few clothes; as he spent the whole day at school, there may not have been time to dry them. It's worth mentioning that water doesn't arrive very often in the community.
>
> *(Maria Esther - ten years teaching)*

Hugging is one of the warmest ways of making a child feel welcome in an environment. A real hug transfers security and makes the other person feel accepted and invited. Carers don't repel children because of their smell, their physical appearance, their stereotype, or other issues presented by their living conditions. What we must reject are the precarious ways in which the majority of poor children in our society are exposed. This is abominable and shameful!

Rejecting a child by separating them from others is one of the cruelest forms of prejudice and exclusion that can exist in the educational context. Rejection cancels out the other. Assuming that education is also a vehicle for the social transformation of the subject, what sense would it make for an educator, a promoter of this change, to distinguish between those who come to her?

Being cautious is part of caring, so that in no situation is the child exported to ridicule or embarrassment. Against these forms of discrimination, those who care welcome and propose possible alternatives for change. When the teacher looked for a reason to give this child an early bath, it was an act of love. She cared for the body and for affection. She taught the child the importance of hygiene and well-being, of touch, of affection; this is a way of educating and developing autonomy, which is essential in this face.

Children are discovering the world, so there's nothing better than learning with care and attention, creating a relationship of love and respect. Seeing Danilo's satisfaction after his bath, teacher Maria Esther recognised that a child's well-being is much more important than complying with a routine; that love for human beings, the value placed on them, is worth much more than the rules and regulations that are sometimes imposed. Flexibility is therefore also important in everyday school life, in the practice of childcare.

At another point in the research, Maria Esther made the following revelation:

- Can you believe that even after almost three years of being Danilo's teacher, when he meets me at school he still comes to hug me, or calls me by name?

Going back to the article quoted, we can see that the psychological aspect of the child is also part of their integral development. The individual cannot go through the process of humanisation and change without taking their psyche into account. When considering this issue, we educators need to be aware of this, not only in the sense of observing, but also educating ourselves so that our actions don't interfere in the child's life in such a way as to develop complications in their relationship with themselves and with others.

Considering that intelligence is a construction, according to Piaget's Constructivist principle, the degree of intellectuality of each child depends on the environment that is provided for them to find ways to bring about this intellectual development. This development and its unfolding depends on the opportunity given to each individual and their experience (PIAGET, JEAN, 2010).

The social aspect, according to Marx's German Ideology, is one of the means by which the individual is inserted and socialises, taking into account their actions, material conditions of existence; a place where they can relate to their fellow human beings, with people from different cultures, customs, habits, ethnicities and beliefs. Living with these differences enables human beings to exchange and acquire knowledge in different ways. As such, socialising is a child's right and also part of their integral development.

But it must be made clear that school and society alone cannot cope with a child's development. There is an African proverb that says: "It takes a whole village to educate a child". He needs a family complement. The family environment is, in fact, the subject's first social means of interaction. It is the family that is the mother educator of the human being. This is independent of our concept of family.

Another complement that contributes to the child's integral development is the community. Community life is also an important vehicle for passing on knowledge and promoting socialisation. In general, this is an informal environment in which people pass on and acquire knowledge from each other. Most of the time, with very few exceptions, this exchange of knowledge takes place orally.

From the definition of early childhood education as the first stage of basic education and its objectives, it is clear that childhood must be thought of responsibly. Therefore, in order to think about an Early Childhood Education project, it is necessary to understand the child, the childhood present today. Or do we still have the same conception of children as a few years ago? According to Miguel Arroyo (1994, p.88): "Childhood does not exist as a static category, as something that is always the same. Childhood is something that is under permanent construction".

By denying childhood as something immutable, stationary, in the quote above, the author suggests that we redouble our attention and care when dealing with and considering today's childhood. If we become aware of this fact, our pedagogical actions will not be static either. This provocation makes us realise the uniqueness of each childhood.

It would be so comfortable for us educators if "childhoods" were "childhood", so we wouldn't need to rethink our planning, our educational actions; we wouldn't need to constantly reframe our pedagogical attitudes and actions. However, teaching practice itself shows us that the author's denial in his quote confirms the plurality of childhood.

If childhood is in constant movement, when we think about it we must also consider our educational actions in relation to this childhood, which is constantly changing and being built. If our teaching moves in line with the child's needs, in accordance with their uniqueness, we won't run the risk of carrying out tasks that are far removed from the reality of the childhood in question.

Margareth Martins de Araújo (2015, p.15) asks: "What to do with the old certainties? At the moment, I feel that they only serve as a starting point, not a point of arrival." If the certainties are old, this tells us directly that there is something new, that we need a new verification in teaching practice. Yes, we can't discard what we've already learned, but we have to realise that certainties are full of uncertainties, and we can't make them our crutch.

The conviction of things should drive us, not paralyse us; it should make us researchers. A researcher is not limited to considering such a discovery as absolute truth. But they are motivated by the restlessness of wanting to know new certainties and realise that as research educators, we must always be vigilant so that these certainties don't make us hampered professionals.

The state's concern for children only began at the age of seven. However, thanks to the Brazilian Constitution of 1988, we have seen some significant changes in the education framework, which have brought benefits to Early Childhood Education. In Section I of Education, art. 208 of this Constitution, in its IV item, according to Constitutional amendment no. 53, 2006 said that it is the duty of the state to guarantee early childhood education in crèche and pre-school until the age of five. And in Article 211, § 2, Constitutional Amendment 14, 1996: "Municipalities will prioritise primary education and early childhood education".

When we become aware of children as subjects of rights, as I've been saying, as educators we have a duty to fight for early childhood education to be a positive milestone in the lives of these children. And by recognising them as subjects of rights, we can't just intervene and offer them anything.

Education needs to make a difference in the daily lives of these children. For this to happen, it is essential that we as educators become aware of our educational actions. Once children have become subjects of law, this right is an obligation of the state. And I believe, as an educator committed to education, that this is also our obligation towards children.

This is not a forced obligation, but something spontaneous, inherent in my choice, when I swore to be faithful to the ethical precepts of my profession. However, in order to ensure that the rights of the child, of childhood, are respected, I, as an educator, need to ask myself what my conception of the child is. According to Mônica Picanço:

> It is therefore up to the Early Childhood Education institution to organise and build its educational proposal, encouraging everyone's participation and constantly evaluating itself, with the aim of guaranteeing all children a fulfilling childhood that reflects the belief in human potential and the value of life (PICANÇO, 2008, p.160).

According to the quote above, in order to ensure the child has a complete childhood that focuses on the credibility of the human being and the value of life, the institution needs to organise and build itself in such a way that its educational proposal encourages the participation of everyone, constantly evaluating itself.

This constant evaluation will enable us to get closer and closer to a more transformative, more equal and fairer early childhood education. This link between educators and children's rights will open up paths that will enable us to fully understand the rights of children, rights that have been historically won.

The credibility that children place in school depends on my relationship with them. If my relationship with the child, who is entrusted to me on a daily basis, is purely authoritarian, then school will simply be a boring place where life has no colour.

However, if my relationship with these boys and girls is one full of human warmth in which human issues and common sense outweigh any kind of discrimination and prejudice, then we will have a generation of students who believe that school is a transformative institution, a means of social transformation.

But for this credit to be given to the school, we can't ignore the fact that the childhood of today is no longer the childhood of yesterday, just as the childhood of children from the privileged classes is not the same as the childhood of children in situations of social vulnerability. And it is these latter children that I intend to talk about in this article, children in situations of social vulnerability.

These children are the ones who depend on the school as a public service. And for them to be guaranteed the right to education, as proposed by the LDB, art. 29 (already discussed). The school needs to recognise the child as a citizen, and the latter as a being with rights, as a being in development. Guaranteeing the integral development of children, of childhood, of boys and girls in situations of social vulnerability is part of guaranteeing their rights as citizens.

## 1. 2. **What early childhood education is for the vulnerable**

I would like to emphasise that the mere age of a child already makes them particularly vulnerable, as they have a high degree of dependency. So every child is vulnerable, no matter what. But in this monographic work, I will be dealing with a specific group of children, belonging to a community located in one of the neighbourhoods of Niterói, Rio de Janeiro.

The fact that these are children in a situation of social vulnerability begs the question: What are these children vulnerable to? From an effective reading of some theorists, scholars, articles and their respective sections, we can reach some common points and understand the real meaning of social vulnerability.

Article 53 of the ECA (Statute of the Child and Adolescent) states that: Children and adolescents have the right to education, aimed at the full development of their person, preparation for the exercise of citizenship and qualification for work, assuring them:

I - equal conditions for access and permanence in school;
II - the right to be respected by their educators, among other items.

We have already seen some of the aspects (physical, psychological, intellectual and social, with family and community support, which imply the integral development of the child). All of these aspects, if well managed, will undoubtedly have an impact on the child's citizenship, providing them with the skills to enter the labour market at the appropriate age.

Do all the families of our poor children, when looking for places for them in public schools, manage to enrol them? And when they do, are they offered the right conditions to stay in school? What is meant by equality of conditions and permanence in school, according to item I of the article we are dealing with in this context? Let's consider these questions! According to Maria Stela Graciani:

> The multiple social, economic and cultural relationships that take place in a society are shaped and regulated by the political organisation that presides over them, according to the interests of the social classes involved [...] (GRACIANI, 2014, p.163).

According to the author, power blocs are used to build relations between the state and society, articulating and confronting economics and politics. In the midst of these, we see children and their rights being dominated and pressurised. The history of social policies in relation to children in Brazil clearly shows us the political and economic interests behind the strategies of articulation between the economic and the political in relation to poor children, considering social inequality to be natural.

Yes, these relationships always move in favour of the interests of a certain section of society, serving a class that is already privileged and maintaining it. Reflecting on these relationships and interests that permeate our society's political decisions, I ask: What place is given to the poor, the working class? Rizzini replies:

> From this point of view, it was up to the poor and dominated to work, and up to the rich and dominant to run society. The discourses and practices relating to policies for children distinguish between the economically and socio-politically disadvantaged and the validated. The former are devalued as a labour force whose survival and school or professional preparation must be at subsistence level, contradictorily validating the project of directing society, of intellectual life, which would fall to the latter. The minimum working conditions for poor children and adolescents seemed to be minimal in the eyes of the factory owners and managers (RIZZINI, 2011, p.34).

Reflecting on the position, the place that the poor occupy in this context, we can surmise what kind of policy is aimed at this section of society. This distinction between the less favoured and the well-off in the elaboration and drafting of political arguments, as well as their execution, leaves no doubt about the neglect and lack of compassion suffered by the former.

The crumbs that have always been given to the poor have never been enough to bring about significant changes in their social, political and economic reality, giving them dignified citizenship. On the contrary, this separation between the classes, which continues to this day, has always pushed our poor and deprived children into the world of work, because the salary conditions offered to their families do not meet their basic needs, forcing their children, at an early age, to cooperate in supplementing the family income. Many, many of these children are exploited by their own families.

In the logic not contradictory to the dominators, but very well thought out by hegemonic politics, it can be seen, according to the quote, that the poor can be offered and pushed through any education project. The education offered to low-income and vulnerable children and adolescents in our country is oppressive, domineering and reproductive. Understand that I'm referring to social vulnerability because, as I said earlier, every child is vulnerable. It is this banking and discriminatory education that is most often offered to them.

Margareth Martins de Araújo (2015, p.100) said that: "Children working to guarantee at least food does not translate into an exception in the world of work. Quite the opposite has been the rule". The author's statement reaffirms how vulnerable poor children in our society are to the denial of basic citizens' rights, such as education, leisure and well-being. She compares the sad reality of children taking part in the financial responsibility of the household to the holocaust.

According to her, the heavy reality of this situation stems from the economic inequality that pervades Brazil, inherited from a slave society. In this context, Martins discusses the failure to comply with Brazilian legislation, which prohibits children under 14 from working. In practice, however, it is not difficult to see the law being flouted. It also draws our attention to the large number of children who work on the streets of big cities, day and night, regardless of their age. They thus turn the paper into a blank sheet of paper, passively accepting it. For Professor Marcelo:

> This kind of work brings children closer to violence. And this violence can turn into criminality. Nobody is born a criminal. That's a fact. Exposing children and adolescents to the streets, however, can make them victims of crime, induce them to commit offences. Child labour can be a great ally, a facilitator for them to move in this direction, towards crime.

> (Marcelo Dias - ten years in teaching)

Once these children are exported to the streets, they are also subjected to their problems, their rudiments. The opprobrium to which they are subjected as victims of the constant violence on the streets makes them invisible to society, to public policies and to human rights. But unfortunately they are not invisible in the eyes of drug trafficking, prostitution, robbery and murder.

It is along this path, the path of crime, that our children, the victims of public neglect, are unfortunately entangled. It's a path that often leads to no return. That's why policies should be about prevention, not just rescue. Prevention has more satisfactory and effective results than remediation. Creating public policies to prevent crime certainly costs less to the public purse than creating policies for recovery.

But until these policies gain traction, our socially, economically and politically marginalised children and adolescents continue to be victims of exploitative child labour, which victimises them and makes them easy prey for crime. One of the means of intervening in this unfair dispute is education, even with its shortcomings. According to Julião:

> The profile of prisoners reflects the section of society that is left out of economic life. They are young, male (96 per cent), poor (95 per cent), non-white (of African descent) and with little schooling. It is believed that 70% of them have not completed primary school and 10% are completely illiterate. Around 60 per cent are between 18 and 30 years old - economically active age - and most of them were unemployed when they were arrested and lived in pockets of misery in the cities (JULIÃO, 2007, p. 23).

We can see from the quote that a frightening percentage of these young people have not had their basic rights respected since childhood. The denial of these rights not only covers the educational sphere, but also the social, political and economic spheres.

The rate of illiteracy among those deprived of their liberty, according to Julião, confirms the denial of a subjective right: the right to education. If the subjects of the EJA suffer the consequences of illiteracy and/or low schooling in adolescence and adulthood, it is because there were violations in childhood, rather than guarantees.

Early childhood education for vulnerable children could only be the same as that which should be offered to all those who benefit from it: quality education that causes significant changes and transformations in the lives and daily lives of individuals. It is essential that social educators are aware of this. The proposal of social pedagogy is for the vulnerable to be included, not excluded, in the practice and proposal of public education policies.

Experience report by teacher Alice:

Once, at a pedagogical meeting, we, the teaching staff of the school, were discussing the school's Pedagogical Project. The discussion centred on the need for the project to be adapted to the reality of the school, in accordance with the local needs of each community. One of the teachers present said the following:

- With the economic crisis, in neighbourhood x, for example, the children of the middle class have been moving into public schools, so the children are *different.*

Another colleague had this to *say:*

- Our clientele has also improved a lot. We already have these children in our school.

If the middle class is coming to public schools, if the clientele is different, where are the excluded, the socially vulnerable? Where have they gone? This is worrying, because since the places are being taken up by "this clientele", "the other clientele" is certainly being disadvantaged. I don't mean that there should be a selection by class to guarantee access to school. The guarantee of education is an unrestricted right.

However, in order for this right not to be guaranteed, we need to pay attention to our pedagogical actions. It's worrying that a teacher considers the fact that the middle class is entering public schools en masse to be an improvement, because there won't be enough places to accommodate this new contingent, without harming students from the less favoured classes.

Since the middle class is considered to be better off, it is inferred that the child who comes from it will be treated differently from the vulnerable child by the educator who considers them to be so. Such a view highlights the exclusion and prejudice between one child and another in education. This complaint is extremely serious! And it clearly shows in whose favour banking education is.

# CHAPTER II

# AMOROSITY AS A PEDAGOGICAL COMPONENT

In this chapter we will look at loving kindness as a pedagogical component in early childhood education; love as an effective possibility for change and transformation in the educational context, not only for boys and girls, but also for educators. Who are the subjects of amorousness? How love can co-operate with school inclusion.

## 2.1 **What is amorousness?**

> *(...) the act of love lies in committing yourself to your cause. The cause of liberation. But this commitment, because it is loving, is dialogical (...). As an act of valour, it can't be cheesy, as an act of freedom it can't be a pretext for manipulation, but a generator of other acts of freedom. Otherwise, it's not love. Only by suppressing the oppressive situation is it possible to restore the love that was forbidden in it. If I don't love the world, if I don't love life, if I don't love people, dialogue is not possible.*

> (Paulo Freire)

It is possible, then, to define amorosity as the expression, the practice, of love. It is in the name of our commitment to the cause of liberating education for the vulnerable in our country that we educators are willing to give love a body, a corporeification, adding it to our struggle. Is it the audacity and courage to fight for education with equal rights for all that makes us loving professionals? Or is it love that makes us bold and brave? I'll leave this question as a reflection for now. From looking to hope, those of us who believe in education as a possibility for change are becoming bold and loving.

When I commit myself to education, I have a cause: children in situations of social vulnerability, for example. If our responsibility as a social educator is to propose an education that frees them from the oppression of hegemonic thinking, that they are doomed to fail, that they are incapable, we need to be loving educators, because without love we will be just another oppressor, or we won't make any difference to that child's school life.

Dialogue is essential for this. When this mutual relationship is established between educator and student, the exchange in the construction of knowledge takes place in a more malleable, more tender way, with more satisfaction, in a more stable way for both parties. I'm not talking about frivolous permissiveness, but about a professional moved by human feeling, a sensitive being, capable of changing their practice through the flexibility inherent in their work, in being an educator. On this path to liberation, I'm increasingly wanting to do right by the student.

The result will be a continuous and progressive process of liberation. This result of loving action leads us to reflections that culminate in listening to the child, perceiving their longings, their anguish, feeling their silence, their fear or their courage, their gaze, their joy or sadness. In this direction, we find meaning in our teaching practice.

We can't be dissuaded from our motivation, from our thoughts, from the education we want and for which we are fighting, we can't be stunned or discouraged by those who attack human rights. The right I'm referring to in this context is the right to release the joy, the love that may be screaming inside you and me, the joy of being who you are, without fear of happiness, without fear of others' envy.

The following is an experience report:

Once, while I was at the table having coffee with some colleagues, I made reference to the children (whom I call my loves, my favours) in my classroom. One of my colleagues interrupted me with the following comment:

- You stand there full of love for them, but one day you might pick up the newspaper and see one of them dead.

(Raquel, nursery school teacher for twelve years)


Calling these children my loves means a lot to me, because it was with this "little group" that I was able to feel for the first time, to experience the flavour and gratitude of working as an educator with children from the working class. Their spontaneity translates into the purity and simplicity of life that we adults often complicate.

The love, care, dedication, attention, all that labour that childhood demands of us educators who work with it, results in this tenderness. That's why they were also my favours. Society and many intellectuals only highlight the suffering, the problems presented by working class children, but experience shows us and teaches us that in this context we also have pearls to cut.

Professor Raquel's speech upset me so much that I left the table at that moment. As I got to know her and some of my other colleagues, I realised that without love we have no hope or any prospect of change, whatever the context. In education, this is doubly important. Society still sees education as a means of social change, still places some hope in it.

For the teacher quoted, however, children who live in communities, who live in situations of social vulnerability, are already condemned to death. So what's the point of investing in these children? They're already ruined, their future is already predetermined, preordained. So what use is my love for them?

In the opposite direction, I have also realised, through sharing experiences with other colleagues, that a simple loving attitude on the part of the teacher can have a profound impact on a child in their school context and bring them a sense of education. Even if they don't realise it now. Being loving is an integral part of overcoming oppression. But we educators also need to be liberated by having love for the oppressed. According to Luiz Schettini:

> What would "affective action" look like in a pedagogical context? There is no manual or roadmap to follow in order to carry out a programme of affective action. This is perhaps the difficulty for most people, even when they understand the importance of affectivity. Acting with affection is the result of everything a person is in their relationships with the world (SCHETTINI, 2010, p. 26).

We thus realise that there is no ready-made answer that defines the expression affective action. What is intrinsic in this context is much more than the planning we have to fulfil or the rules, the "agreements" of everyday life that we create as a pretext to maintain order. The sentimental and professional value is explicit in our attitude.

Our presence and our actions in the classroom have immeasurable significance and value. So let's not let this go unnoticed because we are so caught up in our daily lives. When we realise this, love and affection will only be a consequence. The idea is not for educators to become melancholic professionals. But that we take care not to let sensitivity die, the joy of teaching; because without love, educational practice loses its meaning.

Here's an experience:

Isaque is two (2) years old and was enrolled at the school two months after the start of the school year. When he was handed in by his grandmother, the child resisted crying; the teachers tried to welcome him by inviting him to play. On the first day, during the time he was in the crèche (insertion period - from 8am to 10am), he reacted with a lot of crying, threatening and hitting any adult who came near him. On the second day, Isaac seemed calmer, but he showed aggression when interacting with his classmates, and also when interacting with his playground mates. He would squeeze hard and bite other classmates who approached him, or he would simply approach and bite them. The next day, or the third day, Isaque brought flowers to one of the teachers and hugged her affectionately. We extended his time at school a little more. He ate very well!

From the fourth day onwards, we considered that the child would be able to stay at school full time, as she no longer cried. He ate well and slept well. Little by little, he has shown himself to be very affectionate and helpful, with excellent speech skills and a very sharp intelligence. He has incredible autonomy in carrying out daily activities at school.

However, the child Isaque has been continually signalling to us that he needs help, because in his relationships and interactions with his classmates during play, he has shown signs of aggression, biting and squeezing them, grabbing them by the collar. If he's called to attention by his teachers, he says he's going to kill the classmate he's hit or kicked, and he hits the teacher, calling her low words. Considering Isaque's difficulties, teachers Elisabeth and Cristiane planned to carry out not only collective activities with him, but also individual ones, such as memory games, puzzles, reading, etc.

(Field notebook - June 2016)

Our first reading of this child was that he was an aggressive boy. But fortunately, as soon as we uttered those words we realised our insensitivity; we reworked our reading in time - there were pages left unread. Before any conclusions could be drawn, we needed to know what was going on with Isaac; his attitude was just a reproduction of some context, despite the fact that he was only a few years old. Our relationship with this child could only be a pedagogical and loving one. Our judgements gave way to love. Trying to impose limits on him without any understanding of his reality would be just another form of oppression.

Isaac's mother is seventeen years old and was growing up. One day she went to pick him up from school and spent some time taking him to and from school. During this period we could clearly see a considerable improvement in his performance and in his relationship with the other children. But suddenly, she was no more; Isaac said his mum had gone away. This fluctuation undoubtedly has a direct impact on the child's personal life and his performance at school. Isaque is left in the care of his maternal grandmother.

Through a loving gaze, posture, feelings and actions, we realised that there had to be other ways of intervening in Isaque's daily life, other than in a repressive way. As we searched for alternatives, we realised what an incredible child Isaque was; his difficulties and worries could not be beyond him or our means.

We wouldn't have so many young people and adults in the EJA if, at the very least, children and young people received the necessary support in early childhood education and primary school. But instead of welcoming them, what we see most of the time is their exclusion, be it because of the clothes they wear, the shoes they wear or the way they speak, be it because of where they live or the type of culture they express. The pedagogical activities proposed to them are often exclusionary, due to the lack of contextualisation.

As soon as mechanisms are not put in place to keep a child or adolescent in school, their dreams are automatically fragmented. And if that child isn't taken in by the school, he or she will later have to join the Youth and Adult Education system. This is perverse! It's perverse because if today the child or adolescent already has the right to education, a constitutionally acquired right, why should they have to go to EJA later on? This is because the system is perverse. So we educators also need to free ourselves from this hegemonic oppression.

## 2.2. **The Subjects of Amorosity**

Who are the subjects of loving kindness? In the context of this discussion, we can understand the subjects of amorousness as both the learner and the educator. I understand that love happens in a relationship of exchange, in a mutual relationship. If love can be learnt, you and I, we educators can learn the path of love, as can the student. So we are both subjects of this pedagogical component: loving kindness.

> It is in the loving coexistence with his students and in the curious and open posture that he assumes and, at the same time, provokes them to assume themselves as socio-historical-cultural subjects of the act of knowing, that he can speak of respect for the dignity and autonomy of the learner. It presupposes breaking with conceptions and practices that deny an understanding of education as a gnoseological situation (FREIRE, 1996, p11).

Freire shows us that when the educator assumes a loving coexistence with the student, not only does he/she have a curious attitude, but he/she also allows the student to be the subject of his/her own learning, the subject of his/her own history. This shows respect for the learner and dignifies them while enabling their autonomy.

This complicity paves the way for the student to break away from fear and oppression. In this loving action, we break down and overcome paradigms, concepts and prejudices, not only on the part of the student, but on the part of the educator himself. In this epistemological mutuality, we understand the importance of recognising the student as the protagonist, as the subject of the teaching-learning process in educational practice.

According to Professor Cristiane:

> "It is through affectivity that the teacher-student relationship is constituted; and this enables the teaching-learning process to

become more meaningful to the student."

(Cristiane Moura de Mattos - Teacher for 8 years)

If there is this affective relationship between teacher and student, both are constituted as subjects of amorousness. According to Cristiane, this relationship allows us to see the student as a subject in the process. This bond is based on the fact that the teacher not only teaches, but also learns.

The sensitive attitude of education professionals helps students to be autonomous, motivating them to build knowledge both at school and outside of school. When the teacher's practice is motivated by love, learning takes on a new meaning for the student. Learning with pleasure contributes to the student's performance.

## 2.3. **Love and Inclusion**

For someone to be included in a given context, they need to be heard. Listening is essential in the process of inclusion, because when I listen to the other, I perceive them, they come to exist for me; if they talk to me, it's because I already exist for them. This undoubtedly compromises me. That's why our work should always be followed by dialogue.

According to Paulo Freire (2011, p. 114): "It is necessary, however, that those who have what to say know, without a shadow of a doubt, that they are not the only ones who have what to say." By drawing our attention to putting dialogue into practice, Freire is telling us that for there to be dialogue, I necessarily have to learn to listen to the other person, to what they have to say. A simple act of listening can change your entire lesson plan. Freire proposes an interaction, an internal movement from the other person's speech to his or her thought, committed to communicating, not as a way of making the statement, but paying attention to the questioning, the uncertainty of the person listening. The act of dialogue announces me not only as a critical and questioning educator, but also as a loving, respectful and humble one, in the process of self-evaluating my teaching practice.

As mentioned above, love is dialogical, and if it is dialogical, it is also inclusive. The issue of love as a pedagogical component is of the utmost importance, and therefore essential in the educational process of inclusion. With the exercise of love, consequently the other virtues will follow.

According to teacher Letícia Lucas:

> "Without dialogue, our practice and discourse are empty. Without dialogue, we have no way of knowing how to meet the student's needs. If we don't listen to them, how will we know what they need?"
>
> (Letícia - ten years teaching)

For Leticia, dialogue is a way of being diligent, of avoiding incoherence between discourse and teaching practice. Without this tool, it's not possible to contextualise pedagogical practice with the students' daily lives, and it's just theory. However, if we take the path of dialogue, we are more likely to get it right in our practical experience.

Finding ways and alternatives to include every child who comes to public schools in the school performance process is a way of encouraging them to stay, continuing their education for life and making their dreams possible.

> So I believe that everything depends on how we see the facts; it depends on our training, the authors we choose, our possibilities or limitations to intervene in reality. The act of research is a good exercise in looking at ourselves (Araújo, 2015, P. 47).

According to this quote, the educator's intervention in the everyday life of the child depends on the way they look at the child. In early childhood education, especially, the way this gaze is directed carries greater weight. In this context, the look precedes the word, resulting in actions. The teacher's actions towards their pupil depend on how they see them, whether they are welcoming or exclusionary.

The educator's training, their choice of theory, their possibilities and limitations can determine how they intervene in the role they play in the teaching dynamic. The social educator understands and is aware that he or she is part of the process of changing the paradigms of education, intervening as a transforming part of a society in which the dominated are not only excluded economically, but in all social aspects, above all in terms of quality education, a modifying and liberating education.

As a pedagogical component, loving kindness is directly related to the inclusion of students in the educational sphere. Beyond scientific knowledge, education forms citizens, human beings. Based on this assumption, in this sense, loving kindness plays a fundamental role in this correlation between the student and the teacher.

Research is one of the paths we can follow in order to improve, to mature our loving gaze as a way of including students in our teaching activities. Through research, hypotheses can be raised and/or confirmed, concepts can be changed, certainties and uncertainties can give way to new ways of thinking. What about you, teacher? Do you believe in love as a pedagogical component?

To Mrs Anoil, a teacher who has been teaching for twenty years:

- Through love we conquer, we achieve goals.


If love is such a facilitator, it is also a promoter of inclusion. Loving kindness is a facilitator in the process of inclusion; if you don't love, you don't include. Without being included in pedagogical activities, the student loses stimulation and motivation to learn. Love in the act of educating is a demonstration of the teacher's appreciation of his or her pupil. This concern is essential.

## 2. 4 **What is love?**

The first definition I found is in the thirteenth chapter of the first letter to the Corinthians, in the Holy Bible. The title of this chapter defines love as the supreme gift, and its introduction describes it as an exceedingly excellent way.

> "Now abide faith, hope and love, these three; but the greatest of these is love."
>
> (I Corinthians 13: 13)

From the quote we can see that love really is something sublime, because it is above all gifts, all scientific knowledge, all human eloquence. Despite all these other attributes that a human being may acquire, if love is not the real cause of my fulfilment, it has no value at all. Even if I exercise generosity, distributing all my possessions among the needy; even if I deny my own life, giving it in favour of my fellow human beings, if it is not love of reason, the essence of everything, it will add nothing to me.

Paul ends the chapter by talking about three things that must remain: faith, hope and love. But the greatest of these is love. Faith and hope are interconnected by the motivation they both give to those who put their strength in them. There is no separating one from the other. However, not even faith (something capable of surpassing any human expectation, for those who seize it), can override love. This understanding is found in the apostle Paul's own experience, a man who learnt to love, learnt loving kindness. We can see this in practical terms below.

This experience is related to a slave called Onesimus, cared for by Paul when he was imprisoned in Rome. In the text ONESIMUS - FROM USELESS TO USEFUL, the author explains Paul's letter to Philemon, showing the great change Onesimus had in his life through Paul's love and care. He highlights verses 10 and 11 of the letter, where Paul calls Onesimus his son, and confirms that Onesimus was born in shackles, that he was worthless, but now he is valuable. The text details that Onesimus was once a simple runaway slave, despised by society. However, the verses mentioned, according to the author, clearly show Paul's love, patience and dedication to people, regardless of their social status or level of education (YULAN, DONG, 2016).

In teaching practice, Paul's experience can be applied with the same principle: Love! We can see from this experience that the result came from love as the main component in the process of transformation in Onesimus' life. Therefore, loving kindness is a pedagogical component from which we as educators can intervene in a beneficial way in the lives of children in early childhood education. This intervention can go beyond the walls of the classroom and the school.

The following experience makes us think about the importance of affection in early childhood education, of a loving gaze towards children in situations of social vulnerability:

Currently, the community where the school where the research was carried out is located is going through a major conflict between factions, directly affecting the residents and the functioning of the school, making us hostage to their actions. Both the children and their families, and in some way we educators and other school staff, suffer the consequences of these acts. In dialogue with teacher Cristiane, we came to the conclusion that in the current context in which the children entrusted to us find themselves, not just as professionals, but as human beings capable of caring for others, the best pedagogy we could propose would be welcoming through affection; affection, warmth and human value would have greater significance than any other content. (Field notebook, November 2016)

# CHAPTER III

## What is Social Pedagogy?

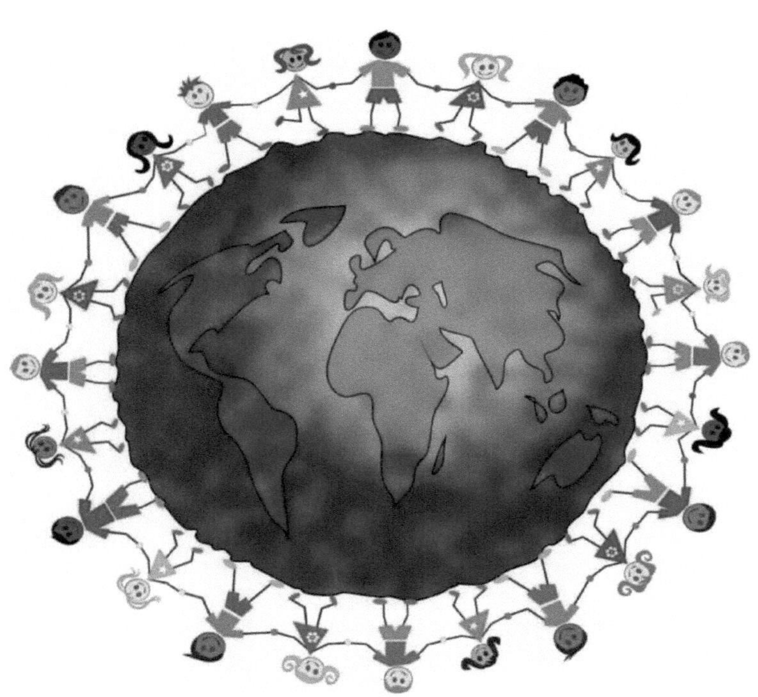

In this chapter, for a better understanding of the work, I intend to present a brief definition of what Social Pedagogy is, and a short description of its aims and objectives, according to Margareth Martins de Araújo (2013). We will also see, according to the same author, the three challenging pillars of the Social Educator.

## 3.1 **History of Social Pedagogy**

According to Margareth de Araújo, in her text "Why social pedagogy", Social Pedagogy is defined as "a component of Pedagogy that is directly responsible for the inclusion of children in situations of social vulnerability in the school universe". From the author's definition, we can see the relevance of social pedagogy in the training of educators.

We therefore understand that Social Pedagogy is not simply defined as a component of Pedagogy, it is committed to those for whom our country's public education policies were not created, are not intended; to those left on the margins of society, forgotten by these policies, which most of the time do not include them.

Social Pedagogy aims not only to point out the diverse needs and shortcomings of the excluded, arising from social political issues. But also to make us realise how much we need to learn from them in order to work with them. That's why Social Pedagogy trains educators to think and reflect beyond educating to teach content alone.

In this same text, the author Araújo reflects that it is for these children, adolescents and young people who are capable, competent and brilliant, but who are not contemplated in the day-to-day running of the school, victims of a process that is not hereditary, but historical, of exclusion, that the social educator has embraced Social Pedagogy.

The following is an experience report:

Once, while teacher Cristiane was introducing the character Chico Bento, from Maurício de Souza's Turma da Mônica, to the class (children aged 2-3), we were interrupted by two-year-old Daniel.

- "Auntie, he's going to beat up his brother."

The character Chico Bento had a hoe on his back. Daniel's words caught our attention because he had always been an observant child, attentive to what was happening in the classroom; he had never shown any signs of violence. However, as soon as he read this, we began to observe him more closely, especially during playtime. His other words and attitudes awakened us to a more sensitive look and listening.

According to Freire (2011), "without the discipline of silence, there is no dialogical communication in the process of speaking and listening". At another point, when we asked the other children in the classroom not to play "pool, pool", Daniel said:

- Only my father can.

We teachers reflected and commented on our observations of Daniel. We concluded that we couldn't naturalise that situation; his signals called for extra attention. Jaume Martinez Bonafé (Universita de Valencia, Spain) said that everyday school life is full of situations that are considered natural and therefore unquestionable. The aforementioned author helps us to understand that systematisation seeks to reflexively deconstruct this naturalisation of the discourse of practice by analysing everyday experiences; he shows us that this so-called naturalisation is a social construction mediated by interests and power relations. He goes on to say that this deconstructive approach allows us to review our perceptions and build alternative and more complex knowledge than that considered natural. It was on this basis that we were able to give Daniel a voice.

In the third part of our observations, we discovered a little more and deciphered the enigma. Daniel hadn't been eating well for a few days. We then spoke to his mother, with whom we established a dialogue from that moment on. During the conversation, he told us that his father was serving time in prison, and when Daniel didn't receive a call from him for a long time, he lost his appetite. We realised that Daniel's father was a reference point for him, as he was attentive and loving towards his son. So, for Daniel, the use of weapons, as well as other everyday practices, is "normal" and should be "cool", because his father is someone good, a good man. "If he's good, what he does is also good". Returning to the author Jaume, he helps us to understand that the epistemological proposal leads us to search for conceptual tools, helping us to reproduce knowledge based on direct action, recognising the character and possibility of a reflective practice, opening the way and enabling critical dialogue with the knowledge already developed; suggesting changes in the social context of intervention. Awakened to this reflection, we continued the dialogue with Daniel's mother, and established the same between ourselves as educators, in order not only to have a sensitive and loving look at Daniel, but also to maintain an action plan so that, as he gained a voice, we could find ways of making possible changes in his daily life.

According to Edgar Morin (1921) "Educating to understand maths or a particular discipline is one thing; educating for human understanding is another". Morin attributes understanding between people as a guarantee of human intellectual and moral solidarity. There is no way to be a social educator who cares about the reality of their students without being a politically correct professional.

If our fight is in favour of these boys and girls excluded by Brazil's policies, then we can't sit back. Conscious political struggle is a form of defence for the excluded and vulnerable in the school context. It is clear that the social educator has one. As educators who are concerned about the rights of the students, for whom the struggle is taking place, we must refrain from alienating education. It is this choice that will tell me who I am working for: an exclusionary and reproductive historical process or an education to change the picture, a humanising education.

> The conception of a genuinely Brazilian Social Pedagogy based on Paulo Freire's pedagogical thinking represents an important contribution to research, analysis and reflection on the rich and diverse practices of popular, community and social education originating from social and popular movements, which are sometimes weakened by a lack of theoretical foundation, marginalised by academia, lacking training facilities and with completely fragmented production without any theoretical or conceptual organicity (SILVA, 2009, p. 8).

According to the quote above, we can see that since the beginning of the history of popular education in Brazil there has been a struggle waged by social and popular movements to ensure that the poorest, least favoured children in our country have access to education through public policies. The struggle is not only to guarantee this access, but also to ensure that this education is of high quality and promotes significant changes in the social, political and economic aspects of the student.

Although the Federal Constitution of 1988 and then the LDB of 1996 and the ECA, include children in some of their articles and sections, with regard to their right to education and their integral development, what we often see is a wide gap between what is in the cold letter of the law and the effective practice of this guarantee by the system, school institutions and educators. Clear changes need to be made in this context.

## 3.2 The Three Pillars of the Social Educator

Returning to the text "Why Social Pedagogy", by the author Margareth Martins, where she affirms the existence of a tripod as a permanent challenge for the Social Educator: the first pillar is the construction of their own identity. The second is acceptance. The third pillar is responsibility.

The first pillar - the construction of the social educator's own identity - only makes sense, according to the author herself, if it is intertwined with the student. If their identity is not linked to the identity of the student, their social work makes no sense. Constructing one's own identity is no easy task, due to the vices we have as a result of the influences suffered in the socialisation process throughout our lives. This identification and intertwining with the student happens through a self-disposal of the ego, recognising the presence of the other and the need for a relationship with that other.

In the second pillar, acceptance, the social educator needs to accept the student with all their historical, social and contextual baggage. But they must first accept themselves. Without self-acceptance, the professional will only be able to speak, to say words without content, without weight. How can educators accept their students if they reject themselves? Acceptance such that it bears witness to itself in reality, dialoguing with praxis in the evocation of coherence.

For headmistress Alice, who has been headmistress for four years:

- The teachers who are most loving towards their children, who best fulfil a friendly relationship with them and their families, are those who are well-resolved within themselves.

Therefore, in order to accept others, social educators need to have love. When we have love for our students, for the task we fulfil for them, breaking through the obstacles of acceptance makes the path less rocky and thorny. The moment we share this love, it's because it already exists within us.

Once we become aware of this existence, when we confront the truth and come up against barriers that try to prevent us from moving forward in this process of acceptance, we will see that it is just another obstacle to overcome. So acceptance, attunement and interaction with the other will simply be a reciprocity in view of an essential internalisation. An internalisation of self-acceptance.

The result and sum is the extension of human relationships. We can see in Alice's speech how important it is to feel good about ourselves, how important this self-transformation is in the process of acceptance. It's a complex and difficult process, but it's necessary when we're seeking changes in the current context. According to Leonardo Buscaglia:

> They can only give what they have. That's the miracle. If you have love, you can give it; if you don't, you can't give it. It's not really about giving, is it? The point is to share. I can share everything I have with you. That way I don't lose what I have (BUSCAGLIA, 2002, p. 17).

The author does not suggest teaching love, or even giving it away, but that we facilitate its progress, that we share it so that it multiplies; for him this phenomenon is learnt, it leads us to be warm and vibrant. Shared knowledge is capable of moving our actions in favour of a dignified education, with quality and respect for the student, because it is not possible alone, we need collectivity, collective action.

Sharing what we have and what we know is not a loss, but a gain. Often the answer we're looking for to a given question lies in the collective. Sharing is adding, because as others take part of what we have, we conquer space, open up paths and expand possibilities.

However, love does not exempt us from the responsibility of equipping ourselves theoretically, nor does it disregard the search for scientific knowledge, for professional preparation. On the contrary, love commits us to the learner, to education. This commitment that educators make is the cause of their generosity. Love is largely anchored to science, to knowledge.

Love generates responsibility. And responsibility is the third pillar presented by Margareth Martins. Once the social educator has built their own identity; from their own acceptance, they accept their students as legitimate, responsibility will only be a consequence. Taking responsibility seriously for their students simultaneously includes them in their pedagogical development. This relationship makes the educator and the student one and the same. Responsibility is linked to the coherence of the social educator. The following is from a teacher

> "Often some mums come in saying that they would have liked to have kept their son or daughter at home, but they didn't because the child wanted to see their aunt at school"
>
> (Cíntia - 8 years in teaching)

Cíntia's speech commits us to early childhood education. If the teacher allows the child to recognise this from an early age, they may have already assumed their responsibility for the childhood entrusted to them. Part of this recognition lies in knowing that their success and the success of the child are closely linked.

In this way, we can see how significant the affectionate memories that children have of their relationship with their teacher are. Intrinsically linked to responsibility, the strings of love built by the social educator demonstrate the link between their discourse and their practice, between their words and their actions.

## Final considerations

At the end of this work, we can see that Social Pedagogy is still a little-explored field. Few authors have written on the subject; most education professionals are unaware of it; there are still few who have or have had any academic contact with Social Pedagogy. We therefore see the need for greater dissemination of this pedagogical component in education, especially in early childhood education for children in situations of social vulnerability.

Social Pedagogy is of profound importance in today's education, helping with research, through the texts worked on and discussed, and through the experience of teaching practice. Through the work I have done, I have been convinced that I need to continually rethink the logic of pedagogical practice and reflect on it, because a new challenge presents itself all the time. Thus, after these reflections, I recognise Social Pedagogy as a path that must be followed.

The concept of childhood that we educators have is outdated. Childhood has changed and we don't even realise that it's not static. We urgently need to review our concept of today's child. What we see is that we are often moving in the opposite direction to the childhood that surrounds us. The pedagogical activities we propose and our actions must always be rethought so that there is no dichotomy between them and today's childhood.

Education for the vulnerable only makes sense if it is the same education that should be for everyone who benefits from it: an education with quality and dignity, and one that brings about changes in their social, economic, political and emotional context, an education for life. Without ensuring their rights in practice, it is impossible to fulfil the legislation. And it is this credibility that you and I place in education, which has historically been denied, but which has now also historically been won, that makes us continue the fight so that in practice this right is increasingly consolidated in favour of the children of the lower classes in our country. I believe that research in this sense is a great ally in making this guarantee a reality.

Early childhood education in the lives of vulnerable families and their children plays a key role in the fulfilment of their dreams and their hopes of improving their lives. Without education, the children of the poor are even more marginalised and have less chance of securing changes in their context. When a mum or dad enrols their child in school, it's because they still have some expectations for them.

Loving kindness as a pedagogical component makes dialogue a facilitating tool in everyday school life. This really is the path to love, a path that some educators have already begun to tread. There are those, however, who want to take this path, but don't dare. Fear is still an obstacle in the lives of many who want to redirect their teaching. Another group, however, is unwilling to change their practices, considering their knowledge to be sufficient; they also claim a loss of authority over the child. Based on this assumption, both educators and students need liberation.

It's a noble feeling to have a loving gaze towards children in kindergarten who are socially vulnerable, and few are able to do so. Learning this way is also a process. This idea of sharing love is fantastic, it's a very rich exchange; in this mutuality there will always be respect on both sides, so there's nothing to be afraid of.

Social educators are important in education because they promote it for everyone, because they are part of the responsibility for including children in situations of social vulnerability in the school context; because they play an important role in building the bridge that Social Pedagogy has been building between the daily practice of popular early childhood education educators and Pedagogy.

When the social educator is faithful to his or her commandments, he or she refrains from any kind of prejudice or discrimination. His identification with the student reveals the meaning of his own identity. Acceptance of the other announces that they are acceptable to themselves, based on the principle that I can only accept the other if I first accept myself. In the responsibility they assume towards their students, social educators confirm the importance of their presence in educational spaces.

# Bibliographical references

APPLE, Michael. **Official Knowledge**. Petrópolis, RJ: Vozes, 1997.

. Curriculum, culture and power. In: **Caderno de Educação. APUBH - I. National Education Congress. Belo Horizonte**, July 1996.

ARROYO, Miguel Gonzalez. **Other subjects, other pedagogies**. Petrópolis, RJ: Vozes, 2012.

. **Curriculum, territory in dispute**. Petrópolis, RJ, 2011.

. **Broken images: trajectories and times of students and teachers**. Petrópolis, RJ: Vozes, 2004.

. The meaning of childhood. In: **SEMINÁRIO NACIONAL DE EDUCAÇÃO INFANTIL**, 1994, Brasília, DF. Proceedings. Brasília: MEC, SEF, COEDI, 1994.

. **Corpo-infância: exercícios tensos de ser criança: por outras pedagogias dos corpos**. Petrópolis, RJ: Vozes, 2012.

ARROYO, Miguel Gonzalez; SILVA, Maurício Roberto da (Org.). Precaritised Bodies That Question Our Ethics. In: **Corpo infância: exercícios tensos de ser criança; por outras pedagogias dos corpos**. Petrópolis: Vozes, 2012.

BENJAMIN, Walter. **Reflections on the child, the toy and education**. Translated by Marcus Vinicius Mazzari. São Paulo: Duas Cidades. Ed. 34, 2012.

BRANDÃO, Carlos. **The Educator: life and death**. São Paulo: Graal, 1983.

BRAZIL. **Constitution of the Federative Republic of Brazil**, Brasilia. 1998.

. **Statute of the Child and Adolescent**. Brasília. 1990.

BRUNER, Jerome. **The culture of education**. Trad. Marcos A. G. Domingues. Porto Alegre: Artmed, 2011.

BUSCAGLIA, Leo. **Love**. Translated by André Feijó. André Feijó. 22nd edition. Rio de Janeiro: Nova Era, 2002.

DE ARAÚJO, Margareth Martins. **Social Pedagogy: dialogues with working children**. VIII. 1. Ed. São Paulo: Expressão e Arte, 2015.

. **Why social pedagogy?** Available at: http://www.projetopipasuff.com.br/revista/editorial.php, accessed on 02 November 2016.

DEL PRIORI, Mary (eds.). **History of children in Brazil**. 6 ed. São Paulo: Contexto, 2007.

FARIA, Ana Lúcia Goulart de. The contribution of Mario de Andrade's playgrounds to the construction of a pedagogy of early childhood education. **Revista Educação e Sociedade**, ano XX, n° 69, December 1999.

. **Preschool education and culture: for a pedagogy of early childhood education**. São Paulo: Cortez Publishing House, 1999.

FREINET, Celestin. **For a people's school**. São Paulo: Martins Fontes, 2004.

FREIRE, Paulo. **Pedagogy of Autonomy: knowledge necessary for educational practice**. São Paulo, Paz e Terra, 2011.

. Creating alternative research methods: learning to do it better through action. In: BRANDÃO, Carlos Rodrigues (Org.). **Participatory research**. São Paulo: Editora Brasiliense, 2006.

. **Pedagogy of hope: a re-encounter with the pedagogy of the oppressed**. São Paulo: Paz e Terra, 2003.

. **Pedagogy of the Oppressed**. Paz e Terra, 32nd edition. São Paulo, 2002.

. **Pedagogy of indignation: pedagogical letters and other writings**. São Paulo: UNESP, 2000.

. **Pedagogy of autonomy: knowledge necessary for educational practice**. São Paulo: Paz e Terra, 1996.

. **Pedagogy of Hope: a re-encounter with the pedagogy of the oppressed**.
Rio de Janeiro: Paz e Terra, 1992.

. **Fear and daring: the daily life of a teacher**. Rio de Janeiro: Paz e Terra, 1986.

. Education and Politics. In: **The Educator: life and death**. Rio de Janeiro: Graal, 1982.

GIMENO SACRISTAN, José. **The Curriculum: a reflection on practice**. Porto Alegre: Artmed, 2000.

GINZBURG, Carlo. Signs: the roots of an indicative paradigm. In:. **Myths, emblems, signs: morphology and history**. São Paulo: Companhia das Letras, 1989.

GOODSON, Ivo F. **Curriculum, theory and history**. Translated by Attílio Bruneta. 11th edition. Petrópolis: Vozes, 2011.

GRACIANE, Maria Stela Santos. **Social Pedagogy**. 1st ed. São Paulo: Cortez, 2014.

HERNÁNDEZ, Fernando and VENTURA, Monstserrat. **Organising the curriculum through work projects: knowledge is a kaleidoscope**. Porto Alegre: Artmed, 1998.

HOBSBAWM, Eric & RANGER, Terencc [eds]. **The invention of traditions**. Translated by Celina Cardim Cavalcanti. Celina Cardim Cavalcanti. 6th edition. São Paulo: Paz e Terra, 2008.

Childhood, history and children in Brazil: approaches and tensions | Lanter. Available at <http: www.revistas.unilasalle.edu.br > Cover > v. 5, n. 10 (2013) Lanter Lobo> Accessed on 02 November 2016.

JULIÃO, Elionaldo Fernandes; SALDANHA, Renan; RIBEIRO, Paulo Fernando. Youth and violence: reflections on data and political perspectives in Brazil. In: **Revista Movimento** - número sobre violência-n°3de2015                            ).
http://www.revistamovimento.uff.br/index.php/revistamovimento/issue/current/showToc

JULIÃO, Elionaldo Fernandes. **The diversity of subjects in youth and adult education** (Mimeo).

KUHLMANN Jr. Moysés. **Childhood and early childhood education: a historical approach**. Porto Alegre: Mediação, 2010.

LÕWY, Michael. **Walter Benjamin: fire warning: a reading of the theses "on the concept of history"**. Trad. Wanda Nogueira Caldeira Brant [transl. of the theses]. São Paulo: Boitempo, 2005.

MICHAUD, Y. **Violence**. São Paulo: Ática, 1989.

MINAYO, Maria Cecília de Souza. **The challenge of knowledge: social research in health**. São Paulo: UCITEC, 2006.

. **Social Research: theory, method and creativity**. 30 ed. Petrópolis, RJ: Vozes, 2011. MORIN, Edgar. The researcher's responsibility towards society and man. In: **Science with Conscience**. Translated by Maria D. Alexandre & Maria Alice Sampaio Dória. Revised and modified by the author. 8 Ed. Rio de Janeiro: Bertrand Brasil, 2005.

MUNARI, Alberto. **JEAN PIAGET**. Translated and organised by Daniele Saheb. - Recife: Joaquim Nabuco Foundation, Massangana Publishing House, 2010.

PRAZERES, Leandro. **See five reasons in favour and five against reducing the age of criminal responsibility**. UOL Notícias Cotidiano, 2015. Available at: <http://noticias.uol.com.br/cotidiano/ultimas-noticias/2015/03/31/veja-cinco-motivos-a-favor-e-cinco-contra-a-reducao-da-maioridade-penal.htm>. Accessed on: 10/11/2015.

PEREIRA, Rita Marisa Ribes and Macedo. Nélia Mara Rezende (eds.). **Childhood in research**. Rio de Janeiro: Nau, 2012.

PICANÇO, Mônica Bezerra de Menezes. Early Childhood Education: a child's place or a student's place? DE VASCONCELLOS, Tânia (org.). **Reflexões sobre Infância e Cultura**. 1ª Ed. - Niterói: EDUFF, 2008.

PILOTTE, Francisco; RIZZINI, Irene (Orgs.). **The art of governing children: the history of social policies, legislation and childcare in Brazil**. 3 ed. São Paulo: Cortez, 2011.

SALLA, Fernando; GAUTO, Maitê; ALVAREZ, Marcos César. David Garland's contribution: the sociology of punishment. **Revista Tempo Social**. vol.18 no.1 São Paulo June 2006.

SARMENTO, Manoel and COUVEA, Maria Cristina Soares de (eds.). **Childhood Studies. Education and social practices**. Petrópolis: RJ, Vozes, 2008.

SCHETTINI, Luiz Filho. Affective illiteracy. In: **Pedagogia da Ternura**. 2. Ed. Petrópolis, RJ: Vozes, 2010.

SILVA, Roberto Da. **Social Pedagogy**. São Paulo: Expressão & Arte, 2009.

. THE RIGHT TO EDUCATION FROM THE PERSPECTIVE OF SOCIAL PEDAGOGY. Available at: www.proceedings.scielo.br/pdf/cips/n4v2/32.pdfIn: Accessed: 02 /11/ 2016

SILVA, Tomaz Tadeu da. **Identity documents: an introduction to curriculum theories**. Belo Horizonte: Autêntica, 2007.

. And MOREIRA, Antônio Flávio. **Curriculum, culture and society**. Rio de Janeiro: Editora

Cortez, 2008. TORRES, SANTOMÉ, Jurjo. **Globalisation and interdisciplinarity: the integrated curriculum**. Porto Alegre: Artmed, 1998.

UNICEF. **ECA 25 years: advances and challenges for childhood and adolescence in Brazil**. Brasilia: UNICEF, 2015.

VASCONCELLOS, Vera Maria Ramos de. **Co-constructivist Perspective in Educational Psychology** / Vera Maria Ramos de Vasconcellos and Jaan Valsiner. - Porto Alegre: Artes Médicas, 1995.

WAISELFISZ, Julio Jacobo. **Map of violence 2015: adolescents aged 16 and 17 in Brazil** (preliminary version). Rio de Janeiro: Latin American Faculty of Social Sciences -FLACSO, 2015 a.

. **Map of Violence 2015: firearm-related deaths**. Brasília: General Secretariat of the Presidency of the Republic National Secretariat for Youth Secretariat for Policies to Promote Racial Equality, 2015 b.

. **Map of Violence 2014: young people in Brazil**. Brasília: General Secretariat of the Presidency of the Republic National Secretariat for Youth Secretariat for Policies to Promote Racial Equality, 2014a.

. **Map of Violence 2014: Homicides and youth in Brazil** (Update 15 to 29 years). Brasília: General Secretariat of the Presidency of the Republic National Secretariat for Youth Secretariat for Policies to Promote Racial Equality, 2014 b.

. **Map of violence 2013: homicides and youth in Brazil**. Brasília: General Secretariat of the Presidency of the Republic. National Youth Secretariat, 2013 a.

. **Map of violence 2013: firearm-related deaths**. Rio de Janeiro: Brazilian Centre for Latin American Studies; FLACSO Brazil, 2013 c.

. **Map of Violence 2012: the colour of homicides in Brazil**. Rio de Janeiro: CEBELA, FLACSO; Brasília: SEPPIR/PR, 2012 a.

. **Map of Violence 2012: children and adolescents in Brazil**. Rio de Janeiro: Brazilian Centre for Latin American Studies; FLACSO Brasil, 2012 b.

. **Map of violence 2011: young people in Brazil**. São Paulo: Sangari Institute; Brasília, Ministry of Justice, 2011. **Map of violence 2006: young people in Brazil**. Brasilia: Organisation of Ibero-American States for Education, Science and Culture -OEI, 2006.

WILLIAMS, Raymond. **Culture**. São Paulo: Editora Paz e Terra, 200.

. **Culture and materialism**. Trad. André Glaser. São Paulo: Editora Unesp, 2011.

XAVIER, Gelta T. Ramos. Inventing traditions and giving meaning to curricular practices. In: NAJJAR, Jorge and CAMARGO, Sueli (eds.). **Education is made (in) politics**. Práxis Educativa Series, No. 6. Niterói: EDUFF, 2006.

**Curriculistas como dirigentes políticos: ruptures with official prescriptions for the curriculum**. Rio de Janeiro: Enelivros, 2007.

YU LAN, Dong. ONESIMUS - FROM USEFUL TO USELESS. In: **Paul's Central Charge**. Daily Food. Series: The central idea of Paul's epistles. 1st ed. São Paulo: Árvore da Vida, 2016.

Printed by Books on Demand GmbH, Norderstedt / Germany